S0-BBO-264

Beacon Small-Group Bible Studies

1 and 2 Timothy, Titus

Beacon Small-Group Bible Studies

1 and 2 TIMOTHY and TITUS

Being Christian in Today's World

by
Jerry Hull

Beacon Hill Press of Kansas City
Kansas City, Missouri

Copyright 1980
by Beacon Hill Press of Kansas City

ISBN: 083-410-6221 (1 and 2 Timothy, Titus)

ISBN: 083-410-6248 (set)

Printed in the United States of America

Cover by: Dave Anderson

Permissions to quote from the following coprighted versions of the Bible are acknowledged
with appreciation:
The Holy Bible, New International Version (NIV), copyright ©️ 1978 by New York Interna-
    tional Bible Society.
Revised Standard Version of the Bible (RSV), copyrighted 1946, 1952, ©️ 1971, 1973.

10   9   8   7   6   (1990)

Contents

How to Use This Study Guide

Before You Begin This Adventure in a
Small-Group Bible Study . . .
Read These Pages of Introduction

God has created us with a basic human need for close personal relationships. This may take place *as you gather in a small group* to apply the Bible to your life.

I. What Should Happen in Small-Group Bible Study?

"They devoted themselves to the apostles' teaching and to the fellowship . . . and to prayer" (Acts 2:42, NIV).

Each group is different . . . yet all should include three kinds of activity—

DISCUSSION BIBLE STUDY
    SHARING EXPERIENCES
       PRAYING TOGETHER

The time you spend in Bible study, sharing, and praying will vary according to the needs of the group. However, do not neglect any of these activities.

The Bible contains God's plan for our salvation and gives us His guidance for our lives. Keep the focus on God speaking to you from His Word.

On the other hand, just to learn "Bible facts" will make little difference in a person's life. To give opportunity for persons to *share* what the truth means to them is to "let God come alive today." Learn to listen intently to others and to share what you feel God's Word is saying to you.

Allow time for *prayer*. Personal communion with God is essential in all fruitful Bible studies. Determine to make prayer more than a "nod to God" at the beginning or end of each session. As members participate in sincere, unhurried prayer—you will be amazed how God's power will meet needs in your group . . . today!

II. How to Begin Your First Session Together

The leader of a new group may wish to prepare name tags with first and last names large enough to be seen plainly.

It is important to order the *Beacon Small-Group Bible Study* guides and give one to each person in your group at the beginning of the first session. Pass out the guides and refer the group to this section of the Introduction. Then ask each person to consider the following:

One thing I would like to gain from sharing in this time together is:

Rank the following in order using number one (1) to indicate the most important and number five (5) the least important.

(   ) 1. Learning to know Bible truths and apply them to my life.

(   ) 2. A chance to begin all over again in my spiritual life.

(   ) 3. To grow in my personal faith in God.

(   ) 4. To deepen my friendships with others in the group as we study the Word together.

(   ) 5. Other purpose _____

Take time to go around the group to introduce yourselves. Then let each member share what he or she would like to gain from this Bible study by filling in the blanks and by discussing this statement: I chose _____

as number one because _____. I

put _____ as number five because _____.

At this point, pause for prayer, asking God to bless this Bible study and especially to meet the needs just expressed by the members of the group.

III. A Key to Success... Make a Group Commitment

What should be included in the group commitment? At the first or second meeting, read the following points, then discuss each one separately.

1. Agree to make regular attendance a top priority of the group.

   Commitment to each other is of vital importance.

2. Where and when will the group meet?

   Decide on a place and time. The place can be always in the same home or in a different home each week, at a restaurant, or in any other relaxed setting. Plan to be on time.

   The time _____ the place(s) _____
   How often?   (   ) Every week
                           (   ) Every other week

3. Decide on the length of the meetings.

   The minimum should be one hour—maximum two hours. Whatever you decide, be sure to dismiss on time. Those who wish may remain after the group is dismissed. Length _____.

4. Decide whether the same person will lead each session, or if you prefer a group coordinator and a rotation of leaders.

   Our leader or coordinator is _____.

5. Agree together that there shall be no criticism of others. Also no discussion

of church problems, and no gossip shall be expressed in the group. Our goal in this Bible study is to affirm and to build up each other.

6. Decide on the maximum number of people your group should contain. When this number is reached you will encourage the formation of a new group. We want our group to grow. Newcomers, as they understand and agree to the group commitment, will keep things fresh. Feel free to bring a friend. Whenever our group reaches an average attendance of _____ persons for three consecutive weeks, we will plan to begin a new group.

Do not become a closed clique. This would eventually lead to an ingrown group. Our goal is outreach, friendliness, and openness to new people.

7. Our time together as a group will be more fulfilling if all of us complete our personal Bible reading before we come together again.

Are group members deciding to make this commitment to personal Bible reading and reflection? _____

8. Decide on the number of times you wish to meet before you reevaluate the areas of your commitment. (Enter below)

MY COMMITMENT TO CHRIST
and THE MEMBERS OF MY GROUP

I agree to meet with others in my group for _____ weeks to become a learner in God's Word.

I commit myself to give priority to our group gatherings, to a thoughtful reading of the Bible passages to be explored, and to love and support others in my group.

Signed _____ Date _____

IV. Guidelines

1. Get acquainted with each other; get on a first-name basis.

2. Each one bring your Bible and keep it open during the study.

3. As you read the Bible passage, each person may ask himself three questions: —What does the passage say?
                —What does it mean?
                —What does it mean to me?

4. Stay with the Bible passage before you. Moving to numerous cross references may confuse a person new to the Bible.

5. Avoid technical theological words. Make sure any theological terms you use are explained clearly to the group.

6. The leader or coordinator should prepare for each session by studying the passage thoroughly before the group meeting, including reviewing the questions in the study guide. In the group study, the leader should ask the study guide questions, giving adequate time for the discussion of each question.

Remember, the leader is not to lecture on what he has learned from studying, but should lead the group in discovering for themselves what the scripture says. In sharing your discoveries say, "The scripture says," rather than, "My church says . . ."

7. The leader should not talk too much and should not answer his own questions. The leader should give opportunity for anyone who wishes to speak. Redirect some of the questions back to the group. As they get to know each other better, the discussion will move more freely.

The flow of discussion in an effective group looks like this:

And not like this:

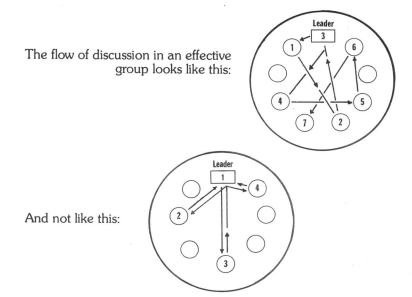

8. In a loving and firm manner maintain the guidelines for the group. Discourage overtalkative members from monopolizing the time. If necessary, the leader may speak privately to the overtalkative one and enlist his aid in encouraging all to participate. Direct questions to all persons in the group.

9. Plan to reserve some time at the end of each session for prayer together. Encourage any who wish to lead out in spoken prayer in response to the scripture truths or personal needs expressed in the group.

Even if you do not complete all the study for that particular meeting, *take time to pray*. The main purpose of group Bible study is not just to cover all the facts, but to apply the truth to human lives. It will be exciting to discover your lives growing and changing as you encourage each other in Christ's love.

A highly effective way to pray in a group like this is "conversationally." "Conversational" prayer includes:

    a. Each group member who wishes to do so tells God frankly what he has to say to Him.

    b. Praying is in a conversational tone—directly, simply, briefly.

    c. Only one thing is prayed about at a time—a personal concern.

    d. Once a group member has introduced his concern, at least one other member, and probably several, by audible prayer "covers with love" their friend's concern.

    e. Then there is a waiting in silence before God. Each person listens to what God is saying to him.

    f. Following the listening period, another member may introduce a personal concern in prayer. The prayer time continues with members feeling free to pray several times.

V. Aids for Your Study

For Group Leaders

You will find helpful, *How to Lead a Small-Group Bible Study*, by Gene Van Note, available from the Beacon Hill Press of Kansas City, Box 527, Kansas City, MO 64141.

For Leaders, Coordinators, and Participants

Bible commentaries should not be taken with you to the Bible study, but it is often helpful to refer to sound commentaries and expositions in your preparation. We recommend:

Beacon Bible Commentary
    Volume 9—Galatians—Philemon

Beacon Bible Expositions
    Volume 10—Thessalonians, Timothy, Titus

It is also helpful to refer occasionally to some general Bible resources, such as:

    Know Your New Testament, by Ralph Earle
    Halley's Bible Handbook

The above resources are available from Beacon Hill Press of Kansas City or from your publishing house.

—This introduction by Wil M. Spaite

INTRODUCTION TO THE PASTORAL LETTERS

1 and 2 Timothy and Titus

When we get a letter, we usually read all of it at one sitting. Paul's letters to Timothy and Titus should be read this way.

Paul, a warmhearted pastor, filled his letters with encouragement, instruction in doctrine, and practical advice for Christian living. He did not have radio and television to communicate his concerns to his younger pastors and their congregations—Timothy in Ephesus and Titus in Crete. But what a help his letters were to these young ministers! And what guidance and encouragement we find in them today as we seek to be Christians in our modern world!

The Young Pastors

Timothy and Titus were close companions of Paul. Timothy was discovered at Lystra (Acts 16:1-3) and was regarded as a son in the faith (1 Tim. 1:2, 18; 2 Tim. 1:2; 2:1). He was with Paul on his missionary journeys and during his imprisonment in Rome (Col. 1:1). He was also sent by Paul on many important missions (1 Thess. 3:1-6; 1 Cor. 4:17; 16:10-11; Phil. 2:19).

Titus was a Gentile convert (Gal. 2:3), led to Christ by Paul himself (Titus 1:4). Like Timothy, he was sent by Paul on many significant assignments in the interest of the growing Church (2 Cor. 8:16-18, 23; 12:17-18; 2 Tim. 4:10).

Purpose and Date

Paul's letters to his young pastors were written to encourage them in the faith and to support them in their responsibilities as leaders in the Church. In both Ephesus and Crete, these two pastors were shepherding a group of Christians surrounded by a vast sea of corruption and paganism.

First Timothy and Titus were written during the interval between Paul's two Roman imprisonments, about A.D. 63 and A.D. 64. Second Timothy was written during Paul's final imprisonment, probably between A.D. 66 and A.D. 67.

NOTE: Unless otherwise indicated, all quoted scriptures are from the *Revised Standard Version of the Bible,* copyrighted 1946, 1952, © 1971, 1973, and used by permission.

In this Bible study, however, we will consider these letters in the traditional order in which they occur in our New Testaments.

It will be helpful for each member of the group to read all three letters in two or more of the modern English translations. These "living letters" are as relevant in our world as in the world of Timothy and Titus.

1   Being Christian in Today's World

1 TIMOTHY 1:1-20

Paul counsels his young pastor, Timothy, and encourages him to refute false teachings and preach the true gospel.

Outline

1:1-7—Introduction
1:8-17—The false and the true
1:18-20—The gospel as committed to Timothy

Open your session with a prayer which requests: openness to God's Word, honesty with oneself, and support for one another.

A. INTRODUCTION

Choose a word or a phrase which you think best describes the nature of life in contemporary society (for example: exciting, falling apart, wicked, etc.).

Share your suggestion with other group members. Is there agreement?
Discuss: What effect does the current state of society have on our attempts to live as victorious Christians?

Sometimes we are tempted to think that this modern day is the worst of all possible times in which to live for Christ. We may be right. Compare, however, the instructions Paul wrote to Timothy and the church at Ephesus. Consider some of the characteristics of this local congregation.

13

The City, Ephesus: Large population; trade and commercial center; location of several pagan religions; and a seaport town. In general: a wicked city which was an alien environment for the gospel of Christ.

The Congregation: All were first-generation Christians; the organizational structure needed improvement; apparently there was considerable difference in the financial abilities of the congregation; and a strong push for false doctrines was being made by some members.

The Leader, Timothy: Young; from a mixed religious background; timid in temperament. He was apparently in less than vigorous health; closely involved with the missionary efforts of Paul; and highly regarded by the great Apostle. (Read Acts 16:1-5; 1 Cor. 4:17; Phil. 2:19-22.)

B. ANALYSIS AND APPLICATION

1. (Read vv. 1-7 in two or three translations.) Paul Told Timothy to stay at Ephesus. List some of the reasons why it might have been tempting for Timothy to leave Ephesus:

List any important assignments (spiritual, family, employment, etc.) which at times you are tempted to abandon. Why were you tempted?

Do you wish to share any experience with the group?

The different doctrine (v. 3) probably refers to either some Jewish fables or false teaching that matter was regarded as evil, so Jesus' appearance in the human flesh was denied.

Describe how v. 5 provides for our day a standard by which to judge whether a teaching is false or true (orthodox).

What is the aim of true teaching?

What is the threefold origin of love? (v. 5)

2. (Read vv. 8-17.) Paul called himself the "worst of sinners" (v. 15). Look again at the list of sinners mentioned in vv. 9-10. Also, reread v. 13.

In what ways could Paul accurately describe himself as the "worst of sinners"?

John Wesley's definition of sin is that it is "a voluntary transgression of a known law." Can you think of a better definition?

Are we less sinful than Paul when we deny the Lordship of Jesus?

3. (Read vv. 18-20.) Paul believed in persistence. Read again his admonition to Timothy in verses 18 and 19a.

How may we gain courage for sticking to a difficult task?

Paul's treatment of Hymenaeus (HY-men-EE-us) and Alexander is severe (read vv. 19-20). What are we to do with people in the church who do not live up to the expectations of the gospel?

Was the banishment of Hymenaeus and Alexander intended for their redemption and thus an apostolic discipline to encourage repentance?

How do we maintain a balance between accepting everyone and yet not allowing false doctrines and wicked living to gain excessive influence?

C. MEMORIZE FOR SPIRITUAL GROWTH

1 Tim. 1:15 (in your favorite translation)
Bonus: 1 Tim. 1:5

D. COMMITMENT TO CHRIST AND TO ONE ANOTHER

Share needs and prayer requests with each other. Pray specifically for each request. Present them to Christ and leave them there.

E. SOMETHING TO THINK ABOUT OR DO

1. Use your newspaper(s). Clip out two or three examples of prevalent attitudes or accepted behaviors which are contrary to Christian principles. Bring to the next session and share briefly.

2. Read 1 Timothy chapter two. Read it in two or three different translations. You will find this practice helpful throughout these studies.

3. *Think Ahead:* In what ways can we regard "submission" as a synonym of "Christlikeness"?

2

Learning to Respect Others

1 TIM. 2:1-15

Timothy receives guidance regarding prayer, worship, and order in the church.

Outline

2:1-2, 8—An exhortation to prayer
2:4-7—The universal call
2:9-15—On Christian womanhood

Opening prayer: Ask God for wisdom and willingness to learn new lessons for personal spiritual growth.

Review your collected newspaper clippings. Briefly summarize last session, "Being Christian in Today's World," and compare the values prevalent in modern society.

A. INTRODUCTION

List important attitudes and behaviors for a husband and wife, or business partners, or neighbors when they are discussing a topic over which they have strong disagreement:

Share your list with other members of the group.

Underline the suggestions made most often. Note: You'll need to use these attitudes and behaviors several times during these studies. Refer to them often.

Some regard 1 Timothy 2 as Paul's instruction for Christians when they worship. Warm-up exercise: Suggest major obstacles to effective worship. (Review later to see if these problems also existed in Ephesus.)

B. ANALYSIS AND APPLICATION

1. (Read vv. 1-2, 8.) Prayer is an integral part of worship. How does v. 1 assess the prayer: "Dear Lord, bless me and my wife, us four and no more— Amen"?

How often do we pray the above prayer; that is, pray exclusively for me and mine?

Is such a prayer always wrong? Why or why not?

Reread vv. 1-2. List the reason(s) stated why we should pray for governmental leaders:

Recall that the authorities of Paul's day were not Christians. He, however, reminded the believers that even such persons were not outside their prayer responsibility. How are we Christians prone to spend our energy and conversation when it comes to politicians and government officials?

Does prayer for those in authority over us prevent us from criticizing or opposing them:

2. (Read vv. 4-7.) We've often heard that we proclaim a "whosoever will gospel." Vv. 4-7 support this universal gospel. Note references to "the truth," "all men," and "a ransom for all."

List the core items of the gospel as enumerated in vv. 4-5:

Focus on two persons (don't mention names). Think of both the most intelligent and the least intelligent person among your acquaintances. Discuss how the gospel of Jesus Christ meets the same needs for both persons:

Share how the formerly used upward pointed "One Way" gesture accurately describes vv. 5-6:

3. (Read vv. 9-15.) "Sexism" and "male chauvinism" call for emotional responses. Recall, however, the exercises in the introduction to this lesson. Many men have used these verses to gain their own advantages, and women sometimes find this passage baffling.

Try to place these verses in the first century Jewish and Greek cultures. Women were subordinate to men. The gospel has emancipated women by giving them equality with men in Christ.

Compare Galatians 3:26-28 with this passage. How do we resolve the apparent conflict in Paul's advice?

Why is submissiveness such a painful lesson for most of us to learn—men as well as women?

How is simplicity (vv. 9-10) related to Christian discipleship?

React: A woman's crown is not primarily in addressing large crowds, but in motherhood (v. 15):

In what ways is the word *submission* a synonym of *Christlikeness?*

How is it that in reading vv. 9-15 we've usually been prone to overlook the positive admonitions to good deeds (v. 10) and faith, love, holiness, and modesty (v. 15)? (Has a prejudiced mind-set prevented a constructive reading?)

C. MEMORIZE FOR SPIRITUAL GROWTH

1 Tim. 2:5-6a (in your preferred translation).

D. COMMITMENT TO CHRIST AND TO ONE ANOTHER (Prayer Time)

Review any needs presented during the scripture study. Identify each concern. Add additional requests. Be sure that a sentence prayer is made in behalf of each need/request. Remember, Jesus invited us to ask, seek, and knock.

E. SOMETHING TO THINK ABOUT OR DO

1. Each morning as you make the final check in the mirror, inquire, "What is my glory—Christ or my carefully prepared appearance?"

2. Keep a log of your "prayers for those in authority." Make sure you spend at least one session each day praying for those persons whose decisions have influence on your life—supervisor or boss, church leaders, and political officials at town, county, state, and federal levels.

3. Read 1 Timothy 3. Try reading it aloud in two different translations.

4. *Think Ahead:* What qualities ought a spiritual leader to possess?

NOTES:

3 Quality Control: Choosing Leaders

1 TIM. 3:1-16

In this chapter the apostle Paul shows his concern for competent leaders for the church and also shares his concepts about the nature of the church and the mystery of godliness.

Outline

3:1-13—Qualifications for leaders
3:14-16—The nature of the church and the mystery of godliness

Open the session with a prayer that we'll not judge each other, but rather will contribute to developing leadership qualities in one another.

How did the experiment of praying for those in authority over you go? Did you feel some resistance to faithfully performing this assignment? Why?

A. INTRODUCTION

Many causes have suffered at the hands of incompetent leaders. Paul desired success for the young congregation at Ephesus. He knew that the alien culture of Ephesus would soon test the quality of Christ's disciples. Exemplary leaders were necessary. Paul detailed the qualifications. Let's see if the requirements remain appropriate.

B. ANALYSIS AND APPLICATION

1. (Read vv. 1-13.) Timothy received instructions regarding bishops and deacons—a "heap o' livin'" is noted in the requirements. What does v. 1 imply about the appropriateness of aspiring for a position of leadership in the church?

Let's not get carried away with the honor, however, until we've checked out the qualifications. List the requirements in two columns below. Read vv. 1-7 and indicate the character and conduct qualities necessary in order to become a bishop:

Character Qualities   *Conduct Expected*

In what ways do the qualifications for a deacon differ from those noted for a bishop (read vv. 8-13)?

(For men) What reactions do our children and wives have if among the believers we are "holy leaders" and yet at home we are no different from worldly fathers and husbands?

When may we conclude that a person has managed his own household well (vv. 4, 12)?

Write in your own words the qualities expected of a deacon's wife (v. 11):

2. (Read vv. 14-18.) The Pastoral Epistles (1 & 2 Timothy, and Titus) reveal the warm personal concern of a spiritual father. Paul's commitment to these new Christians punctuates each sentence. In this paragraph he states his intention of visiting soon. In the letter he assures them of his interest and advice until he comes.

What does Paul state as the purpose for this letter (v. 15)?

List and briefly discuss the meaning of the three titles Paul assigns to the fellowship of Christian believers (v. 15):

Some key elements of Christ's coming to earth are enumerated in v. 16. List each one below:

In what ways is it adequate to say that the essence of our religion is Jesus? How is it inadequate?

To what extent is our behavior, as modern-day Christians, determined by the nature of Christ Jesus and by our relationship to Him?

What portion of our behavior seems to be primarily determined by the standards of our unchristian society?

How do we maintain a proper balance between these two?

C. MEMORIZE FOR SPIRITUAL GROWTH
1 Tim. 3:16

D. COMMITMENT TO CHRIST AND TO ONE ANOTHER
Recall as many as possible of the prayer requests made so far during these sessions. Add names of two or three important spiritual leaders and pray especially for them. Finally, pray that each group member will be able to discern his/her spiritual leadership roles.

E. SOMETHING TO THINK ABOUT OR DO

1. Each day, during your devotional period, review the list of qualifications necessary for bishops and deacons. Daily ask God to help you measure up to the responsibilities you must fill.

2. Read 1 Tim. 4:1-16. This is a great "Family Passage." Read and discuss the chapter with your children, especially teenage young people.

3. *Think Ahead:* What can children and teens teach adults about Christian living?

NOTES:

4

Discipline or Punishment

1 TIM. 4:1-16

Because of their damage to the church, Paul alerts Timothy to false teachers. Then he challenges the youthful pastor to be a good minister of Jesus Christ and to be an example to all.

Outline
4:1-5—An alert to false teachings
4:6-16—A good minister of Jesus Christ

Let's focus our opening prayer on self-assessment. Ask God to use this passage of scripture to help us determine our level of spiritual fitness and to choose plans for increased spiritual discipline.

A. INTRODUCTION

Physical fitness intrigues many. Thousands of us are jogging toward eternity. Spectatorism, currently, must yield to an increased emphasis on participation.

Many athletes learn that a championship depends upon the willingness to deny oneself of detrimental pleasures.

Do some of the same disciplines apply to one's religious behavior? How austere or rigid must we be in order to prove that we have our bodies under Christ's domination?

Gnosticism (nos-ta-siz-um) was a view held in the early Christian centuries that matter, including our bodies, was evil. Asceticism was one natural outcome of the Gnostic (nos-tic) error. Asceticism, while not a common word, describes a major religious response throughout the centuries. Ascetics (a-set-ics) believe that spiritual benefit comes to an individual as a result of extreme self-denial.

Do we have any examples of asceticism in today's church? Illustrate:

B. ANALYSIS AND APPLICATION

1. (Read vv. 1-5.) Some Christians at Ephesus insisted that the physical body was evil and thus a hindrance to Christian life. They attempted to resolve this dilemma by recommending that the evil body be deprived of desired pleasures.

Which pleasures are mentioned on the taboo list (v. 3)? Reactions?

How did Paul challenge this error (vv. 4-5)?

Can you list anything that God has created which is not good?

Are there no restraints in the Christian life? Are we free to enjoy everything we may desire? Why?

How does the phrase "received with thanksgiving" establish boundaries on desires we are free to satisfy (v. 4)?

The first paragraph of chapter 4 presents two important uses of the word *faith*. (1) Faith is a relationship with God entered into by accepting Jesus as Lord; (2) Faith is the body of doctrine that constitutes true Christianity.

Paul unmasked the false doctrine of distorted asceticism with some rather strong expressions. List the particulars of Paul's criticism (vv. 1-2).

2. (Read vv. 6-16.) The second portion of this chapter presents a corrective for the false teaching Paul discovered in the young congregation. He denounced the false doctrines which would punish and deprive the human body. He quickly added, however, discipline as a necessary balance.

How might we explain the current "physical fitness" craze that's sweeping our society?

List some of the "in" physical fitness activities:

Discuss: What is the relationship between physical fitness programs and spiritual growth?

Describe the payoffs we might expect if we train in godliness (vv. 8-10):

Physical exercise often increases our ability to resist unsuitable behaviors and emotions. Identify the problem Paul implied will be resisted by spiritual training (v. 7, also, compare v. 3):

Several commandlike statements, in vv. 11-16, remind us that spiritual discipline must characterize our lives. List the request Paul made in each of the following verses:

v. 11

v. 12

v. 13

v. 14

v. 15

v. 16

To what extent do Paul's advices for young Timothy apply to the young today (v. 12)? (Remember: "Young" in the New Testament time referred to one who was of military age—up to 40 or 45 years):

C. MEMORIZE FOR SPIRITUAL GROWTH

1 Tim. 4:7b-8 (in your favorite translation)

Bonus: 1 Tim. 4:12

D. COMMITMENT TO CHRIST AND TO ONE ANOTHER (Prayer Time)

Review prayer requests that have come up in the discussion of the scripture. Add other requests which anyone wishes to share. Select someone to pray specifically for each request. End your prayer time with a thanksgiving prayer for the way God is going to work in each situation.

E. SOMETHING TO THINK ABOUT OR DO

1. Throughout the week review your "spiritual fitness" program. Plan new ways of improving your efforts for spiritual growth. Share your plans at the beginning of the next session.

2. Read 1 Tim. 5:1-25 in two or three modern English translations.

3. *Think Ahead:* What is the Christian's responsibility for the disadvantaged or dependent in the church? In society as a whole?

NOTES:

5   Who Cares? A Christian Congregation

1 TIM. 5:1-25

The apostle Paul now shares practical advice for the care of church families. Also this chapter counsels us on honoring leaders of the church.

Outline
5:1-16—Responsibilities toward church families
5:17-25—Responsibilities toward the elders of the church

Let's open this session with a prayer that God will make us sensitive to the needy, and to ways that we can help: the lonely, sick, dependent, elderly, hungry, poor, and those discriminated against.

Quickly review from the last session goals we've set for a more effective spiritual fitness program.

A. INTRODUCTION

Television specials and news reports probe our comfortable and small world. Not too far from us we can discover a great number of hurting people. A long list of problem situations comes quickly to mind *when* we allow ourselves to think of those who need help.

Why is it so *easy* for us to almost never think about the genuinely needy in our society?

How does our belief in the value of work and the importance of self-initiative affect our attitude toward dependent people?

Paul desired a full ministry for Timothy and the church at Ephesus. Earlier the apostle instructed the congregation how to behave as members of the household of God (3:15). Some elements of their task are related in this chapter. Here we learn that: (1) There are needy among us; and (2) We are responsible for their care.

Paul was particularly concerned about the needy widows in Ephesus. Now, as then, there are persons whose circumstances make it almost impossible for them to take care of themselves.

List some of today's dependent or disadvantaged groups; those who are unable to make it without assistance from others:

B. ANALYSIS AND APPLICATION

1. (Read vv. 1-16.) Paul refers to "real widows" (vv. 3, 5, 16). List below the factors Paul considers necessary in order for one to be described as a widow worthy of financial help from the church.

Note vv. 8 and 16 in order to determine whose responsibility it is to care for widows. State below:

In Paul's time a widow found herself in a difficult financial predicament. Perhaps many of today's elderly (males as well as females, singles as well as marrieds) would receive Paul's attention.

Show how vv. 3-16 provide us clues for caring for the elderly among us:

Exactly what was (is) the congregation's responsibility for the dependent:

Ephesian Widows (then)   *Elderly Persons (now)*

Paul makes requirements of the widows who deserve the care of other believers. What are some of the attitudes and/or behaviors that ought to characterize such persons (vv. 3-16)?

What shall the congregation do if widows of Ephesus, or dependent elderly persons of today, fail to display the proper attitudes or behaviors?

Describe what v. 8 says about our roles as parents, children, or other close relatives.

2. (Read vv. 17-25.) In the first half of chapter 5, Paul exhorted care for the dependent—those disadvantaged by the events of life, over which they had no control. Now, he adds the congregation's responsibility of caring for its elders. First, worthy widows, now, worthy elders. Usually, the terms "elder" and "bishop" are used as synonyms by Paul. Review material in 1 Tim. 3:1-7 regarding qualifications for a bishop.

Perhaps *church leaders* is the best way to express today what Paul means in this chapter when he refers to *elders*. The church leaders include both salaried and volunteer persons. What does the congregation owe them? Let's see Paul's recommendations.

What do vv. 17-18 suggest regarding some church leaders (elders) being employed by the congregation?

Do these verses (17-18) imply that some church leaders (elders) are more worthy than others?

What is the wisdom (or importance) of the counsel stated in v. 19?

Illustrate how today's congregations may still need to use the guidelines of v. 19. What problems may result if this safeguard is ignored?

Summarize in a phrase or short sentence the main point of vv. 19-22:

Verses 22, 24-25 form a single unit of thought. How, according to these verses, do we know when a person is qualified to become a church leader (elder)?

How well does the proverb, "Chickens come home to roost," communicate the meaning of vv. 24-25? Why?

Add to Paul's list. How do church leaders (elders) earn and hold the respect and confidence of the congregation?

A lot of uses, noble and otherwise, have been made of v. 23. It appears that Timothy was a total abstainer. Paul worried about Timothy's health. The phrase, "a little wine for the sake of your stomach," is not a central theme of the chapter. It does, however, raise some age-old questions about the use of medications. What types? How much? What if drug-dependency develops?

C. MEMORIZE FOR SPIRITUAL GROWTH
1 Tim. 5:8

D. COMMITMENT TO CHRIST AND TO ONE ANOTHER

List every request that has been indicated during the session. Go around the circle and ask each person for prayer requests either for themselves or others. Prepare to spend several minutes in prayer in support of one another. Then pray that each of us shall yield ourselves and our needs to a loving Heavenly Father.

E. SOMETHING TO THINK ABOUT OR DO

1. During the week make two lists which will help you to analyze how well your congregation is keeping the guidelines that Paul established in chapter 5. First, identify the needy and dependent being served by your congregation. Second, identify other disadvantaged persons whom it is possible your congregation might be able to serve:

2. Read 1 Tim. 6:1-21. Use several translations in order to increase your understanding.

3. *Think Ahead:* How much money must we have before we can begin to live a "life-style of generosity"?

NOTES:

6   Instructions for Affluent Christians

1 TIM. 6:1-21

In this final chapter of his First Letter to Timothy, Paul seems to crowd in everything he had failed to write about earlier. His concern for Timothy and the church emerges forcefully in this full package of counsel.

Outline

6:1-2—Duties of slaves and masters
6:3-10—Unwise teachings and the peril of wealth
6:11-16—Rewards of holy living
6:17-19—The stewardship of wealth
6:20-21—The stewardship of the gospel

Open the session with several sentence prayers of thanksgiving. Give special thanks for the many comforts and pleasures we enjoy.

Review the care-giving efforts of your local congregation. Share any possible new areas of service that were identified.

A. INTRODUCTION

"Money talks" they say. According to this perspective, money guarantees success, wins elections, sways opinions, and may be traded for goods and services which we need or enjoy. Those with the fewest dollars have the least influence, the smallest number of options, and fewer advantages.

May we conclude, then, that possessing considerable money is more virtuous than having little or none? In this chapter Paul meddles deeply into our motivations for getting money and into our spending priorities. Let's study his close review of our love affair with cash.

B. ANALYSIS AND APPLICATION

1. (Read vv. 1-2.) The employer-employee relationship dominates most of our lives for at least 40 hours per week. Paul noted that being a Christian influences how we either supervise others or take orders from them.

Relate how, in your experience, Christians make better bosses, or better employees.

How did becoming a Christian affect your role as employer or employee?

The Christian gospel contained the eventual destruction of the slavery system. However, Paul taught that while the system continued a Christian must remain ethical in his slave-master relationships.

What were the specific advices Paul recommends for the slave and master (vv. 1-2)?

Slave   *Master*

What applications might these verses have for today's employer and employee when both are Christians?

2. (Read vv. 3-10.) "What's in it for me?" Could it be that we ask this question before almost every decision? Paul reminds Timothy that many choose Christianity (godliness) because they see it as a means of gain (v. 5).

What might be some selfish motives for one to become a Christian?

Compare Matt. 6:33 with v. 6. What assurance may we base on these two verses?

Paul must be kidding with us in v. 8. Right? How can we explain this verse in light of how we affluent Christians live?

Paul portrays a desire to be rich (v. 9) and a love for money (v. 10) as dishonorable motives. List his reasons (vv. 9-10).

React: Some people claim to have as their "gift" the ability to make money:

Contrast the emphasis of v. 11 with Paul's discussion in vv. 6-10:

3. (Read vv. 11-16.) This paragraph sets a high expectation for us. We can understand concern about money; but, in your own words, what is the point of Paul's high goal in vv. 11-16?

"Fight the good fight of faith" (v. 12) generates many ideas. How might this advice be understood when we recall that Timothy was young, Ephesus was wicked, and false teachers wanted to mislead the congregation?

Do you ever feel that remaining faithful is a lot like a fight? Is it okay to feel this way?

List the characteristics of our Lord Jesus which Paul enumerated in vv. 15-16:

4. (Read vv. 17-19.) This paragraph provides instructions for affluent Christians.
How rich are we when we compare ourselves with previous generations and with the people of most countries in the world?

Paul notes several commands for "us rich folks" (vv. 17-18). List them:

How can we change our pattern of behavior to become rich in good deeds, liberal and generous?

Can a person become too generous?

What are the rewards for generosity? (v. 19)

5. (Read vv. 20-21.) Even Paul's closing remarks contain two "final licks." Indicate them below and note the relevance of these instructions for modern Christians:

1.

2.

C. MEMORIZE FOR SPIRITUAL GROWTH
1 Tim. 6:7-8 (in your preferred translation)
Bonus: 1 Tim. 6:10

D. COMMITMENT TO CHRIST AND TO ONE ANOTHER
Review the evening's discussion for any needs that have been expressed. Go around the circle for any additional concerns and requests. Reread vv. 16-17 to be reminded of the nature of the One in whose name we pray. Spend several minutes in prayer together.

E. SOMETHING TO THINK ABOUT OR DO
1. Review your time budget and money budget. How much generosity is planned? Can you devise ways of increasing efforts of generosity?

2. Read 2 Tim. 1:1-18.

3. *Think Ahead:* Do my deeds (actions) reflect my faith in God?

7   Loyalty: An Indispensable Quality

2 TIM. 1:1-18

This Second Letter to Timothy is Paul's last letter. It was written during his final imprisonment in Rome, amid the dreary limitations of his confinement.

In spite of his own unpleasant situation, Paul is more concerned for Timothy and the future of the gospel than he is for himself. Though he knew that death was near, Paul's spirit was strong and his faith victorious. We are fortunate that this last expression of his faith is ours to read and enjoy.

Outline

1:1-2—Paul's love for Timothy
1:3-7—A tribute to Timothy's heritage
1:8-14—An adequate gospel to proclaim
1:15-18—God is faithful

Begin with a prayer of thanksgiving for friends and for your brothers and sisters in Christ.

A. INTRODUCTION

We cherish our final moments with a departed friend or loved one. We often recall, "I remember the last thing she said to me was . . ." Those final moments and last words are precious.

Paul's Second Letter to Timothy belongs to the "last words" category. The Epistle rings with notes of urgency and finality. Paul is once again imprisoned in Rome. He projects no hope of being released, and much talk about suffering is found here. In the fourth chapter, Paul announces his eternal victory in Christ.

Paul, we often wonder how much stronger the Church of the Lord Jesus Christ might have been had you been given at least one more year, or perhaps even five more. But we can't fret over what might have been. We simply want to say "thanks" for the miles traveled, the sermons preached, the arguments waged against heresies, the churches established, and the letters written. You indeed provide for all of us a model of Christlikeness.

We hope that Timothy was able to reach you and deliver the cloak, the books, and the parchment before that last winter (4:13). You deserved that final kindness. Probably, however, you would be more delighted to know that a small group of us are gathered today to study your Second Letter to Timothy so that we also might "fulfill our ministry" (4:5) in the closing decades of the changing, confusing 20th century. We love you, Paul.

B. ANALYSIS AND APPLICATION

1. (Read vv. 1-2.) Paul's greeting to Timothy is both official and personal. His authority as an apostle is claimed, but not at the expense of warm affection for his son in the gospel, Timothy.

Paul regarded his apostleship to be by the will of God (v. 1). To what extent are people today being called by the will of God for specific tasks?

What are guidelines to be followed if one is to learn God's will for his or her life?

2. (Read vv. 3-7 in two or three translations.) The salutation of ancient letters was often followed by concern for the welfare of the recipients. Paul follows that pattern here. In doing so he provides information about Timothy and his relationship with him.

Evangelistic efforts among nonreligious people is very important, but the seed of the gospel seems to root more easily if there has been spiritual training in one's rearing. Read 1:5 and 3:15 and compare with today. What percentage of our congregation is comprised of people who were reared in Christian homes? _____ %

What does this percentage say about the congregation?

How do we pass on the faith to our children and grandchildren (v. 5)?

How can we live with ourselves if our children do not turn out to be a "Timothy" (that is, do not keep the faith)?

Verse 6 implies that our responsibilities in places of leadership come as a:

Some ways we might revive or rekindle the gift of God for spiritual responsibilities are:

Describe some current situation in your life for which v. 7 is just the right remedy or prescription:

3. (Read vv. 8-14.) In v. 12 Paul briefly states, "This is why I suffer." What is the explanation for his sufferings (v. 11)?

What is Paul's reaction to suffering (v. 12)?

Verse 8 sets a challenge for Timothy. What is expected of him?

Paul gives Timothy some instructions for dealing with suffering. What are the instructions (vv. 13-14)?

What counsel may the 20th-century Christian take from these verses in order to deal with hardships?

Does it work? Give an incident of how the grace given us in Christ proved to be sufficient in your life.

What two possessions has Christ given us (v. 14)?

1.   2.

How important for victorious living are these two indwelling possessions (v. 14)?

4. (Read vv. 15-18.) Paul was very human. Amidst all the glowing passages of Christian victory found in 2 Timothy we find this paragraph. What
elements of humanity like our own do you detect in this section?

Paul recalled many who had obstructed his attempts to proclaim the
gospel. He also remembered some who had abandoned him. Among the
many faithless, however, one faithful individual stood out. His name was
Onesiphorus (*On*-uh-*sif*-o-rus). Scarcely a household name, but Onesiphorus's one-line act on the stage of history was noble. He was a friend that
stuck closer than a brother.

Onesiphorus's name meant "profitable." In the agony and loneliness of
his final days Paul was sustained by the courageous loyalty of this faithful
man.

Few, if any, of our brothers and sisters in the Lord are in the extreme
circumstances in which Onesiphorus found Paul. However, list the name of
some person, and the circumstances, to whom you can be Onesiphorus.

Onesiphorus risked his life, perhaps even lost it (4:19), in search for and
regularly visiting Paul. Think of some modern-day risk-taking loyalties dis-
played by Christians.

If history should give you a one-liner remembrance, at this point in
your life, what do you think it might be?

C. MEMORIZE FOR SPIRITUAL GROWTH
2 Tim. 1:7

D. COMMITMENT TO CHRIST AND TO ONE ANOTHER

Paul cherished his memories of Timothy and Onesiphorus. Christian brothers and sisters in life's desperate moments represent the very face and presence of God to us (compare Matt. 25:35-40). May we be just that to one another as we pray today. When we remove our masks, some of us have very heavy burdens weighing on us. We need each other. Help one another carry your burdens to Christ.

E. SOMETHING TO THINK ABOUT OR DO

1. "Who needs me?" Let that question be continually on your mind this week. Be Onesiphorus to somebody.

2. Read 2 Tim. 2:1-26.

3. *Think Ahead:* How does a Christian determine what is truth or reality?

NOTES:

8   How to Be a Strong Christian

2 TIM. 2:1-26

Timothy is challenged anew to be a good soldier—a disciplined soldier of the Cross. He is to accept the discipline of suffering which shall not be in vain. He is to hold fast to the truth in the face of dangerous error. He is to understand the identity and security of the Church of Jesus Christ.

Outline

2:1-7—By all means be faithful
2:8-13—Through death to life
2:14-19—Avoid dangerous false teachings
2:20-26—In patience and love

Begin your session with a prayer for strength and courage in the Lord. Honestly acknowledge both the difficulty of your circumstances and the grace of the Lord.

Review last session's "Something to Think About or Do." Invite several to share their efforts to be "Onesiphorus" to someone.

A. INTRODUCTION

Fetters used to bind criminals, bound Paul. His crime was preaching the gospel (vv. 8-9). "Suffering" was more than an academic subject for the apostle—the end had come. Yet here Paul exhorted young Timothy to "be strong in the grace that is in Christ Jesus" (v. 1).

Paul is my kind of man. A man in prison, certain that he will not be released except by a martyr's death, deserves the right to talk about suffering. Some of Paul's human gloom surfaces in this letter, but even now he is interested in the churches, their leaders and the furtherance of the gospel.

B. ANALYSIS AND APPLICATION

1. (Read vv. 1-7.) We aspire for strength; a person with power can get things done. Sometimes, however, we find ourselves in a dismal limiting predicament, powerless to alter the circumstances. What was Paul's instructions for such a situation (v. 1)?

According to v. 1, what is the source of our strength?

What difference does it make in our circumstances to be strong in the grace of the Lord Jesus?

Paul instructs Timothy to entrust teaching to what type of individual?

This "entrusting" business raises the issue of delegating leadership to others. To what extent does our congregation, or subgroups within it, illustrate the folk wisdom, "If you want a job done well, do it yourself"?

Why is it hard to release duties (honors?) to our fellow believers?

What one major spiritual principle do you think Paul is illustrating by his reference to a soldier, an athlete, and a farmer (vv. 3-7)?

How can we maintain singleness of purpose today with all the demands that are placed upon us?

2. (Read vv. 8-13.) Staying with a hard task calls for great nerve and assurance that the reward will compensate for the cost. In this paragraph, Paul appears to reflect upon the agony of his situation in comparison with the absolute faithfulness of God.

Three contrasts bring God's faithfulness to our attention:
    a. v. 8—Jesus was dead, but
    b. v. 9—I am wearing fetters, but the Word of God
    c. v. 13—If we are faithless, He

What are some ways that we as individuals, or as a congregation, partially fetter the Word of God?

Give some examples of our faithlessness which has been conquered by God's faithfulness.

3. (Read vv. 14-19.) Appropriate teaching that leads to purity of life is primary in Paul's instruction to Timothy. The teaching and life requirements are uniquely blended in this paragraph. Paul gave Timothy, the Ephesians, and indeed all of us, several specific commands in these verses.

Identify these commands:

v. 14

v. 15

v. 16

v. 19

Why are we so often undisciplined (inattentive) to careful study of the Scriptures?

What are some suggested corrections?

Verse 17a provides a frightening suggestion. Indicate ways in which talk may have gangrenelike qualities in today's congregation:

4. (Read vv. 20-26.) An average household uses many containers—everything from fancy copper and fine china to torn paper sacks. Paul uses two illustrations to show that only high-quality containers belong in the household of God. The Church of the Lord Jesus has no place for cheap vessels (members) given to profane babbling or uncontrolled passions of youth. Rather, members of the household of God must be what (v. 21b)? State in your own words.

Throughout these Pastoral Epistles Paul reminds us that we are to be containers fit for receiving the gospel (review 1:12). How do we become vessels worthy of the glorious gospel and the indwlling Holy Spirit?

Read 1 Cor. 6:19-20. Doesn't this make you feel like a noble vessel?

Verses 24 and 25a cite several qualities that ought to characterize the Lord's servant. What are they?

How do we eliminate from our behavior the tendency to be quarrelsome?

C. MEMORIZE FOR SPIRITUAL GROWTH
2 Tim. 2:15
Bonus: 2 Tim. 2:24-25a

D. COMMITMENT TO CHRIST AND TO ONE ANOTHER
Listen carefully and lovingly to each other's requests. Pray that each of you might be strong in the grace of Christ—whatever the difficult circumstances you may be facing.

E. SOMETHING TO THINK ABOUT OR DO
1. Between class sessions observe carefully your relationships with others. Record each time that you are quarrelsome—or tempted to be—and why.

2. Read 2 Tim. 3:1-17. You will find it helpful throughout these studies to read the scripture passages in two or three translations.

3. *Think Ahead:* How important is the Bible for 20th-century Christians?

NOTES:

9   Aliens in an Alien Society

2 TIM. 3:1-17

The last days of the gospel dispensation will be characterized by corruption and persecution. But Timothy, and all believers, are reminded that they have invaluable resources in the example of devout Christians and in the inspired Word of God.

Outline
3:1-9—Courage for difficult times
3:10-17—The believer's invaluable resources

Let several pray to open your session, the focus of the prayers being, "Lord, lead us to know and follow Your truth."

Invite several to share their Quarrelsome Quotient (QQ) as experienced since the last session.

A. INTRODUCTION

In the United States "aliens" must register once each year. The annual announcement makes me feel uneasy. Somehow it seems unfortunate that anyone is excluded or "rounded up" and painfully reminded that they don't really belong.

Paul, however, implies that Christians also are aliens. We do not fit in the wider society. We are citizens of another Kingdom. Because we must willingly accept our status as "aliens," Paul probes our alliances. In this chapter he raises the questions, How comfortably do we fit into this present age? and Why?

B. ANALYSIS AND APPLICATION

1. (Read vv. 1-9.) The "signs of the time" are not always easily understood. We often fail to detect all the clues and thereby make faulty decisions. Paul wanted Timothy to understand the characteristics of the last days. In vv. 1-5 he lists 20 characteristics of people in the last days.

Select the five you think are most apparent in our day. Share them with the group.

a. _____ (v. ___)   d. _____ (v. ___)
b. _____ (v. ___)   e. _____ (v. ___)
c. _____ (v. ___)

What does Paul's instruction, "avoid such people" (v. 5b) mean for us today?

How are we to regard the popular designation, "the last days"? May we regard the term as the period between Jesus' ascension into heaven and the Second Coming? Discuss.

How often do we appear to be more in love with pleasures than to be lovers of God (v. 4)?

What are the ways in which we give evidence of going through the form of religion without revealing any of God's power in our lives (v. 5)? Why?

Paul's tough stance against false teaching is revealed by reference to Jannes (Jan-eez) and Jambres (Jam-breez). Tradition holds that they were Egyptian magicians who opposed Moses. Paul affirms what their outcome will be. What is the final result of false teachings (v. 9)?

Even though truth will ultimately prevail, great harm often occurs in the meantime. Teachers of a counterfeit faith often enjoy a measure of success. Read again vv. 6-8.

What influence will teachers of false doctrines likely have on lonely, bored, and unfulfilled people? Why?

Provide some current illustrations of the impact of false teachers upon impressionable people.

What can we learn from groups outside of the orthodox church about winning people?

How are vv. 1-9 a challenge to the popular idea of the "common decency of all men"?

2. (Read vv. 10-17.) Paul makes a frightening reference in v. 7. He notes that some people seem to have an ability to sort through the evidence but never finally to select the truth. What are the possible defenses for such persons?

The two corrections to false teaching are: (1) Exemplary lives (good models of Christian living); and (2) the Holy Scriptures. These two guides will serve all of us well—even the most impressionable or the most suspicious.

Do all Christians have the right to do as Paul and say, "Look at me and the life I live" (v. 10)?

Why should all Christians strive to become as exemplary as Paul?

WARNING. Exemplary lives involve costs. What price did Paul pay (v. 11; compare Acts 14:1-23)?

What do you make of v. 12? Is the case overstated?

In what ways have we modern Christians obtained immunity from persecution through compromise with the world?

React: Every person who follows Christ fully will find himself/herself in conflict with certain elements of our secular society.

The Scriptures are able to make us wise about Christ and to instruct us how to enter and live in a personal relationship with Him. We may be confident how we should live in these last days.

According to vv. 15-17, what will the Scriptures do for us?

What will these effects of the Scriptures (cited in above answer) do for the person who encounters false teaching?

How do we keep a proper honor for the Scriptures without falling into the trap of "worshipping" them?

The Scriptures are sacred because of their "servant role." They don't point out only carefully stated rules. To whom and to what do the Scriptures point?

How might the last phrase of chapter 3 be regarded as a summary of what a study of the Scriptures ought to accomplish in our lives?

C. MEMORIZE FOR SPIRITUAL GROWTH
2 Tim. 3:16-17

D. COMMITMENT TO CHRIST AND TO ONE ANOTHER
Review any requests that have already been expressed in the discussion. Special prayer attention might be given to three things: *(a)* Persons we know

who are victims of false teaching; *(b)* Our congregation so that we might be strong enough to resist false teachings; and *(c)* A compassionate prayer for the genuine salvation of those who teach false doctrines.

E. SOMETHING TO THINK ABOUT OR DO

1. Identify types of false doctrines which are strong in your community. Also, determine what efforts various congregations may be using to overcome these teachings.

2. Read 2 Tim. 4:1-22. Try reading it aloud to some other person.

3. *Think Ahead:* How should we live so that when the time comes we can die well and confidently?

NOTES:

10

Christians Die Well

2 TIM. 4:1-22

This final chapter of Paul's letter contains a solemn charge to Timothy. It also records an aged prisoner's final testimony and an expression of his loneliness. The letter gives Paul's last words to his son in the faith.

Outline

4:1-5—A charge to preach the Word
4:9-18—Testimony and personal requests
4:19-22—The aged prisoner's last word

Pray for a special sense of the presence of the Holy Spirit as you enter into this Bible study.

Share anything that has been especially significant to you from the previous lesson.

A. INTRODUCTION

"Soon we'll be done with the troubles of the world" summarizes well the spirit of this final chapter. The end has come. Paul knows it. He appears almost hurried. The old warrior imparts a final charge, gives a last testimonial to the keeping power of God, and offers some final personal instructions.

One feels the weight of the task being transferred from Paul to Timothy. A new runner must now carry the torch.

B. ANALYSIS AND APPLICATION

1. (Read vv. 1-5.) Paul spares no words. He makes his instructions emphatic. In a short space he collects a lifetime of ministry and hands it to Timothy.

What one word or phrase communicates the spirit of Paul's final charge to young Timothy (vv. 1-5)?

How might we also catch the sense of urgency with which Paul charges Timothy?

What factors tend to cool our "red hot" urgency about the gospel of the Lord Jesus?

Paul believed that zealous performance by Timothy and his congregation would be an effective deterrent to false teachings. How might zealous living still be a powerful deterrent to false spiritual groups?

How strong a motivation is the fear of the judgment of God (v. 1; compare 2 Cor. 5:10-11)?

What might it mean in our day for us to "always be steady" (v. 5, RSV)?

2. (Read vv. 6-8.) This paragraph is precious to all who believe in the Lord Jesus. Paul assured Timothy that a life of faithfulness to Christ is both possible and satisfying. In these three verses he reflects for one final moment on his pilgrimage. Then he fixes our gaze on his triumph in Christ.

We are to be a sacrifice both in life (Rom. 12:1-2) and in death (v. 6). How do these sacrifices (pouring out our lives as a gift to God) differ?

Death meant departure for Paul. What are some things from which Paul would be released by death?

What are some things from which we'll be freed by death?

In what ways is it permissible to look forward to death as "rest from all this frettin'"?

Is the concept of fighting a battle a correct description of life? How can life be regarded as a struggle?

How do these verses support the overworked phrase, "Do your best, that's all anyone [including God] can expect"?

In what way are all of us included in v. 8?

3. (Read vv. 9-18; see "Pronunciation Guide" at the end of this chapter.) The human frailties of an exhausted campaigner are evident in these few verses.

Identify some of the emotions Paul might have been experiencing as indicated in vv. 9-18.

Is it appropriate for a mature Christian to experience discouragement? Why or why not?

What things most often lead Christians to discouragement or depression?

How do the following verses help us understand some ways of dealing with discouragement?

v. 9

vv. 17-18

Read the following three New Testament references to Demas: (1) Philem. 24; (2) Col. 4:14; (3) 2 Tim. 4:10. When read in this order, what clues do we get about spiritual backsliding?

4. (Read vv. 19-22). Paul's global and all-encompassing passages (for example: 1 Corinthians 13; Romans 12; Philemon 2) have thrilled Christians throughout the centuries. However, Paul's life, as for all of us, was lived out in particular places in the company of specific individuals. Verses 9-22 of this chapter distinguishes some of his associates and records the infamy of others.

The references to Paul's many colleagues in the gospel presents a basic reality about human nature—our need for each other.

How many people among your acquaintances are always strong and have no need for companionship and assitance from others?

Since none of us can claim complete self-sufficiency, why, then, do we find it so difficult to admit weakness, discouragement, or indecision?

How did Priscilla and Aquila contribute to Paul's life? Read Acts 18:2-30; Rom. 16:3-4; and 1 Cor. 16:19.

What did Onesiphorus do for Paul? Read 2 Tim. 1:16-18.

Who are some valued helpers who have ministered to you? Write their names and share some incident(s) with the group.

C. MEMORIZE FOR SPIRITUAL GROWTH
2 Tim. 4:7-8

D. COMMITMENT TO CHRIST AND TO ONE ANOTHER
In these extremely personal letters Paul revealed his need of others. Make this mutual dependency the focus of your prayers. Go around the circle

with prayers of thanks for one another. Also continue your prayer time by praying specifically for the requests of each member of the group.

E. SOMETHING TO THINK ABOUT OR DO

1. Keep the faith—continue your personal relationship with the Lord Jesus and hold firmly to a pure and strong doctrine.

2. Read Titus 1:1-16 in several translations.

F. PRONUNCIATION GUIDE

Demas (*Dee*-mas)
Thessalonica (Thes-uh-lo-*ny*-cuh)
Crescens (*Cres*-sens)
Galatia (Guh-*lay*-shah)
Titus (*Ty*-tus)
Dalmatia (Dal-*may*-shah)
Tychicus (*Tick*-ih-cus)
Ephesus (*Eff*-ih-sus)
Troas (*Tro*-as)
Carpus (*Car*-pus)
Prisca (*Pris*-cah)
Nero (*Knee*-row)

Aquila (Aw-*kwill*-a)
Onesiphorus (On-uh-*sif*-o-rus)
Erastus (E-*ras*-tus)
Trophimus (*Trof*-ih-mus)
Miletum (Mi-*lee*-tum)
Eubulus (You-*boo*-lus)
Pudens (*Poo*-dens)
Linus (*Ly*-nus)
Claudia (*Claw*-dia)
Timotheus (Ti-*mo*-the-us)
Ephesians (Uh-*fee*-shuns)

NOTES:

11 The Gap Between Words and Actions

TITUS 1:1-16

The letter to Titus is similar to those that Paul wrote to Timothy. Here, too, we have the counsel of a veteran to one of his younger pastors. In this first chapter we learn the reason for Titus going to Crete and we hear Paul stress again the qualifications of a minister of the gospel.

Outline
1:1-4—Greetings from the apostle
1:5-16—The purpose of church organization

Let's begin this session with a prayer for the "gaps" in our lives—the gap between what we are and what God wants us to become; and the gap between what we pretend, and how we actually live.

A. INTRODUCTION

Review Acts 28:30-31. What happened to Paul at the end of v. 31? Many have assumed that this two-year period was followed by Paul's death. However, another strong tradition concludes that Paul was released from prison and spent a few more years establishing churches, preaching, and teaching. During this time of freedom Paul wrote the letters of 1 Timothy and Titus. Later, he was imprisoned in Rome for a second time. It was during this brief second imprisonment, followed by death, that Paul wrote 2 Timothy.

Titus was charged with overseeing the work of the young churches on the island of Crete. Anti-Christian influences surrounded these young churches comprised of new Christians. Paul wrote Titus instructions for the growth of the baby Christians and the development of the young churches.

The Cretan Christians were only one step removed from paganism. Paul wanted to guarantee that they would not relapse into their old ways. How do the dangers of relapse (or backsliding) differ for those of us in a "Christian culture" and who come from a line of many generations of Christians?

B. ANALYSIS AND APPLICATION

1. (Read vv. 1-4.) The letter begins with a long and somewhat complicated greeting. Careful analysis, however, reveals some very simple and powerful thoughts.

Paul both identified himself and stated the authority which gave him the right to send correspondence. What two titles did Paul give himself?

(1) _____ (2) _____

Is there a conflict between these two titles? What was Paul attempting to claim by calling himself both a "servant" (slave) of God and an "apostle" (messenger or envoy)?

The gospel of the Lord Jesus is first and simply "eternal life" (v. 2). Christianity involves both a creed (proper beliefs) and a moral call (proper behavior). Its primary essence, however, is partaking of the eternal life of God. Read John 11:25-26. What do these verses tell us about eternal life?

"The preaching with which I have been entrusted" (v. 3) is a phrase rich with meaning. How does this verse describe the proper mood for anyone who preaches or teaches the gospel of the Lord Jesus?

2. (Read vv. 5-16.) These verses reveal Paul's deep anxiety over the strength of the several congregations in Crete. The Letter to Titus testifies that neither spiritual growth nor defeat of false teachings will be accidental. The congregations must deal resolutely with these matters.

Congregational life is not only warm smiles, congenial handshakes, and love feasts. Sometimes, according to Paul, strong action must be taken so that the gospel will not be compromised. How do you regard the strong commands of "amend what is defective" (v. 5, RSV), "confute those who contradict it" (v. 9, RSV), "they must be silenced" (v. 11, RSV), and "rebuke them sharply" (v. 13, RSV)?

Describe any modern circumstances which require similar vigorous action on the part of congregational leaders:

How can negative sanctions be taken without splitting the congregation?

When, according to these verses, is it appropriate to censor and when is it appropriate to be patient a while longer with those who are damaging the congregation?

Review 1 Timothy, chapter 3, for a discussion of church leaders. The verses in this paragraph remind us that high qualifications are placed upon a would-be church leader. For example, note the requirements listed in verse 8:

1. _____   4. _____
2. _____   5. _____
3. _____   6. _____

How does a congregation prepare people to occupy places demanding such high expectations?

What if we've goofed? What do we do (in Christian love) if a present leader does not measure up?

Verses 11 and 13-14 affirm that what one teaches is of extreme importance. Reread these verses. How do they speak to the popular idea: "It doesn't make much difference what one believes as long as he is sincere"?

How would Paul (or, how do you) regard the assertion that Jesus Christ is only one of many pathways to ultimate truth and eternal life?

How often do we find ourselves included in the "they" of this verse? "They profess to know God, but they deny him by their deeds" (v. 16, RSV).

What are some of the ways in which we tend to deny God by our deeds?

Sometimes "doubt" is suggested as the opposite of faith. Perhaps v. 16 instructs, however, that "disobedience" is actually the opposite of faith. Compare the purpose of this Letter as Paul states it in the first verse. ". . . to further the faith of God's elect and their knowledge of the truth which accords with godliness, . . ." (v. 1).

How might we do a better job of translating our knowledge of God into godly deeds?

C. MEMORIZE FOR SPIRITUAL GROWTH

Titus 1:16a

D. COMMITMENT TO CHRIST AND TO ONE ANOTHER

Allow sufficient time for various items of praise or need to be expressed. (Don't worry about moments of silence.) Make prayers of thanksgiving first and then follow with prayers of request. Give special thought to praying for wisdom and courage for your congregation's leaders.

E. SOMETHING TO THINK ABOUT OR DO

1. Work on at least one gap in your life. Attempt to eliminate the gap between what you say and what you do in one specific area.

2. Read Titus 2:1-15.

3. *Think Ahead:* Is it fair to measure the soundness (orthodoxy) of a group's doctrine by the Christlikeness of their lives?

NOTES:

12   Christianity Changes Our Conduct

TITUS 2:1-15

In this chapter Paul gives conduct guidance for believers of all ages and classes. He gives also the meaning of Christ's coming and the basis of our hope for His return.

Outline
2:1-10—For Christians of all ages
2:11-15—Salvation and hope

Change sometimes causes pain. Open this session with a prayer asking God to make us open to criticism and change.

Give opportunity for several members of the group to share their efforts, during this past week, at eliminating some gap(s) from their lives.

A. INTRODUCTION

The old-time camp meeting preachers often observed energetic demonstrations of shouting and aisle-running in the crowds where they preached. I still remember the wisdom of one such preacher as he affirmed, "It isn't how high you jump that counts, but how straight you walk when you come down." This man of God understood the implications of the gospel.

The Christian faith interferes with the way we live. A relationship with Christ "cramps my style."

Paul exhorted Titus to make this same point clear to the Cretan congregations. He instructed Titus to remind the believers that they must live so that they adorn, or show the beauty of the gospel of the Lord Jesus.

B. ANALYSIS AND APPLICATION

1. (Read vv. 1-10 in several translations.) One's age, sex, or status makes no difference when it comes to righteous living. Males, females, young, old, strong, and free are all expected to live in a way that honors God. None can weasel out and exclude themselves from the demand to exhibit deeds which reflect our personal relationship with God.

Paul identifies five categories of persons in this section. List the five groups which are commanded to live by the constraints of the gospel (vv. 2-10):

1. _____   4. _____
2. _____   5. _____
3. _____

Verses 2-10a might be regarded as an application of the main thought stated in v. 1 and 10b. The sense of the section might be stated by placing a free paraphrase of these two portions together:

"But tell them the kind of life which ought to result from sound doctrine . . . that they may adorn (beautify) the gospel of God our Savior" (vv. 1, 10b).

What is (are) the common theme(s) for moral living expected of the four age-groups (vv. 2-6):

How might these expectations be applied to the sex and age groupings in today's congregation? In what ways are the instructions still relevant?

1. Older men   2. Older women

_____   _____
_____   _____
_____   _____

3. Younger women   4. Younger men

_____   _____
_____   _____
_____   _____

Paul is speaking directly to Titus in vv. 7-8. What is Titus asked to model for other church leaders?

Do opponents of Christianity have some bad things they can truthfully say about the quality of Christian life they see in me and our congregation (v. 8b)? If so, what?

Substitute "worker" or "employee" for the word *slave* in v. 9. List the qualities of a Christian worker as found in vv. 9-10:

Since some will never read the Gospel According to Matthew, or Mark, etc., how might your life as a member of the labor force be regarded as "The Gospel According to You"?

Self-control might be the central quality necessary to achieve the numerous expectations Paul makes in vv. 1-10. How do we gain Christian self-control?

2. (Read vv. 11-15.) Self-control seems difficult. It is difficult unless we remember the true nature of the gospel of Christ. Thus the demands for moral conduct (vv. 1-10) do not depend upon our puny efforts, but rather are based on the grace of God which we've received. In this paragraph Paul summarizes, for Titus and his congregations, the gospel of Jesus Christ.

Who or what event is referred to in v. 11?

According to v. 12 what are the reasons for Jesus being sent among us?

A backward look to the coming of Jesus is recommended in v. 11. A forward look to the return of Jesus is noted in v. 13. These are mentioned to inspire us to "live godly lives in this present world." What guideline comes to mind when you consider living a godly life?

Does a godly life ever seem boring? Hard? Irrelevant? Why?

What are the reasons, cited in v. 14, why Jesus died for us?

What emotional reactions are triggered when you think about being (1) redeemed from all iniquity?

(2) made part of a zealous people who are eager to do what is good?

How important did Paul regard Titus's task of teaching Christian conduct (v. 15)?

How different would our congregation be if we come a little closer to Paul's "grab them by the lapel" teaching style as he suggests in v. 15?

C. MEMORIZE FOR SPIRITUAL GROWTH
Titus 2:14

D. COMMITMENT TO CHRIST AND TO ONE ANOTHER
Let's pray especially for ourselves and for one another. We want to pray also for persons outside the group, but sometimes it seems God expects so much! In this study we've been reminded that (1) our conduct should be above criticism and (2) our major passion should be to do good deeds in the name of Christ. We need prayer.

E. SOMETHING TO THINK ABOUT OR DO
1. Plan to share one or two thoughts with the group at its next session. Relate (a) a moment when you felt God expected you to change some behavior or perform some deed, and (b) share your feelings—did you feel submissive? Unfairly pressured? Otherwise?

2. Read Titus 3:1-15. Reading in two or three different translations may be helpful.

3. *Think Ahead:* What is the Christian's source of both personal goodness and inspiration for good deeds?

13   The Christian in Society

TITUS 3:1-15

The final chapter is filled with instructions as to what Titus should teach —and what he shouldn't teach. Paul stresses the duty of Christian citizenship and gives counsel regarding the importance of consistent living in this present world. Faith and works were not to be separated.

Outline

3:1-8—Christian duties in a pagan society
3:9-11—Avoid unprofitable controversies
3:12-15—Some final instructions

Open the session with a prayer that focuses upon Jesus' gift of himself for us. Perhaps some poetry or a song about His sacrifice will help prepare us for a study of the Word.

Have several members share their recorded moments as instructed in the last session. What were the reactions when we felt God made a specific demand upon us?

A. INTRODUCTION

Christians hold dual citizenship. We belong to God's eternal realm and anticipate the joys of heaven. We dare not, however, pretend that we are free from obligations in this present world. In this paragraph Paul both celebrates the glory of eternal life and insists on Christian conduct in the nitty-gritty of the everyday.

B. ANALYSIS AND APPLICATION

1. (Read vv. 1-8.) Titus and the Cretan Christians received guidance for living in their society. List the specific instructions given in vv. 1-2:

In what ways is the following admonition relevant for Christians in our generation, "Be ready for any honest work" (3:1c)?

Is there an impossible compromising of principles stated here? Paul declares that we must be submissive to evil authorities (v. 1) and speak evil of no one (v. 2). How do we follow this advice when there is so much corruption in various levels of government?

How do we distinguish between an honest, accurate appraisal of a person's performance and "speaking evil" about him (v. 2)?

Rate yourself on a scale of 1 to 10 with "10" representing complete gentleness and perfect courtesy to all men (v. 2) and "1" a total absence of courtesy:

My score: Why?

Paul's letters to Titus and Timothy place great stress on right thinking and right living. However, Paul refuses to be trapped in robotlike religion. He affirms again and again that the basis of salvation is our life in Jesus received through faith. Verses 4 through 7 provide one of Paul's summaries of the gospel. Let's review these words in loving faith.

How is Jesus described in v. 4?

Are we saved because of our works, or is there another reason (v. 5)?

What two results of being saved by Jesus are stated in v. 7?

1.
2.

In v. 8 Paul writes, "I desire you to insist on these things" (RSV). What are the "things" to which he is referring?

Relate how salvation in Christ (vv. 4-7) produces the proper conduct desired throughout this letter:

2. (Read vv. 9-11.) Teaching may be disruptive and misleading. One potential danger is identified here, namely, teaching that produces nothing but cheap talk. Both the Greeks and the Jews were fascinated with words. We moderns are much like them—we have opinions and arguments about everything. We love to hear ourselves talk.

Why did the Cretans, and why do we, find it more exciting to *talk* about kindness and good deeds than actually doing these things?

React: "A discussion which does not result in action is largely a waste of time."

What options might I choose if my opinions of some biblical or theological issue differ from everyone else in the group?

What did Paul recommend that the congregation do with a factious or divisive person (v. 10)?

Wasn't Paul a bit harsh? What other alternatives do we sometimes try with a highly opinionated person? What has this done for the congregation?

3. (Read vv. 12-15; see "Pronunciation Guide" at the end of this lesson.) Paul informs Titus that he may expect one of two persons as a replacement (v. 12) and that he himself should come to Nicopolis for the winter.

Paul appears to close his letter with haste; however, he cannot help but make a couple of additional instructions about generosity. What does he ask to be done (vv. 13-14)?

1.

2.

Paul raises the frightening possibility of an unproductive life (v. 14). How is such a life avoided?

C. MEMORIZE FOR SPIRITUAL GROWTH
Titus 3:5

D. COMMITMENT TO CHRIST AND TO ONE ANOTHER
Prayer together and for one another is essential. Make the most of these moments. Why not give special prayer for those in authority and those who are divisive? Also, listen carefully to the personal requests of each other.

E. SOMETHING TO THINK ABOUT OR DO
1. Make a list of ways you might be more effective in your witness to the society in which you live.

2. Share with others the blessings you received through these small-group Bible studies.

F. PRONUNCIATION GUIDE
Artemas (*Ar*-te-mus)   Apollos (A-*pol*-los)
Tychicus (*Tick*-ih-cus)   Cretians (*Cree*-shuns) (KJV)
Nicopolis (Ni-*cop*-o-lis)   Cretans (*Cree*-tans) (modern English)
Zenus (*Zee*-nus)   Macedonia (Mass-ih-*do*-nia)
Grace be with you all. Amen (Titus 3:15).

For information about additional Beacon Hill Press of Kansas City individual or small-group Bible study guides, contact your local bookstore or write directly to the publisher,

Beacon Hill Press of Kansas City, MO 64141-0527

NOTES:

NOTES:

NOTES: